How to SURVIVE the SATs Writing Tests

- You've got TWO writing tests to do for the SAT.
  For each one you've got to do a different type of writing.

- There's a whole bunch of different types of writing that could come up. This book gives you practice for a load of them. The rest of them are in the other workbooks.

- The fancy flap at the back of this book has got the Rules for each type of writing. When you start a question, fold out the flap and read through the rules for the writing you're doing.

- Each question in this book gives you a writing grid for planning — just like the real SAT tests. We've stuck in ideas to get your brain working. Read our ideas and then come up with ideas of your own.

- Pick the best ideas, plan your writing and write it — then make a bazillion quid by selling it to Hollywood. (This last bit is optional)

Are you going to Writing Wonderland or Writing Blunderland?

How it all works — what teachers need to know...

Year 6 HAVE to do SATs, whether they like it or not

Writing's one of the toughest things kids have to do in the SATs.
We think they'll do better if they understand exactly what they're being asked to do.

In our **Writing Rules** book we explain how to do each type of writing that could come up in the SAT and give clear examples of how to get it right.

The **Workbooks** give kids loads of **practice** on all the types of writing covered in **Writing Rules**:

WORKBOOK 1 — FICTION WRITING

- HORROR STORIES
- ADVENTURE STORIES
- FABLES
- STORIES WITH FLASHBACKS
- FANTASY ADVENTURES
- PLAY SCRIPTS
- STORIES WITH A FAMILIAR SETTING

WORKBOOK 3 — NON-FICTION WRITING

- FACTUAL REPORTS
- LETTERS TO FRIENDS AND FAMILY
- FORMAL LETTERS
- ADVERTS, FLYERS
- DIARIES
- DISCUSSING ISSUES
- WRITING ABOUT YOUR POINT OF VIEW

WORKBOOK 2 — FICTION WRITING

- STORIES THAT RAISE ISSUES
- MYSTERY STORIES
- CONVERSATIONS
- HISTORICAL STORIES
- SCIENCE FICTION STORIES
- HUMOROUS STORIES
- STORIES WITH A DILEMMA
- STORIES WITH A TWIST

WORKBOOK 4 — NON-FICTION WRITING *(THIS BOOK)*

- WRITING AN ARGUMENT
- RECOUNTING EVENTS
- ARTICLES
- BIOGRAPHIES
- NEWSLETTERS
- INSTRUCTIONS
- DESCRIPTIONS
- EXPLANATIONS

Here's how it works...

1) Make sure the whole class knows that:
   - the point of this book is to GET INTO WRITING WONDERLAND and stay in.
   - you stay in Wonderland by <u>meeting targets</u>.

2) Use the 'Writing Rules' book to go over the style of writing you want to cover.

3) Read through the question. Get the kids to use the boxes on the left-hand page to generate ideas, then plan their work using the writing frame on the right.

4) Set the kids targets for writing up their answers. You can base them on the rules printed on the folding page at the back of this book. We've left a space where you can write the target at the bottom of each right-hand page.

5) If a child meets their target, they're in Writing Wonderland, but if they miss one they go to Writing Blunderland — until next time they meet their targets.

6) You could circle the Wonderland or Blunderland picture at the top of each page to show whether they've met their targets.

7) Even better, make a massive poster, with stickers for the kids' names. Stick the names in Wonderland or Blunderland in a weekly ceremony. Give prizes for going to Wonderland and punishments for going to Blunderland — maybe trimming all the grass at the local park with nose-hair trimmers, or, more realistically, doing the page again for homework...

Section 1 — Writing An Argument

Writing An Argument — 1

*Arguing in the SAT isn't like arguing with your little brother
— you've got to be polite and formal for a start...*

You read a quote in a newspaper which says:

"All children are mindless idiots who watch too much television and have no idea how to behave. If I had my way they would all be put in the army, as it didn't do me any harm." (Mr D. Green)

Write a reply to the editor, arguing against the views in the letter.

You will need to decide:
- What points you will make to argue against Mr Green
- What facts to include to back up your argument

Think about your argument and scribble down extra ideas in the boxes below.

WHAT YOU DON'T LIKE ABOUT MR GREEN'S QUOTE

- he thinks we watch too much TV
- says children are mindless idiots

FACTS SHOWING KIDS AREN'T MINDLESS IDIOTS

- study for difficult SAT exams
- work hard at school
- know loads about computers

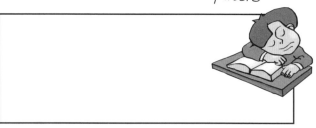

EVIDENCE THAT KIDS BEHAVE WELL AND DON'T WATCH TOO MUCH TV

- me and my friends prefer playing sport to TV
- a lot of kids do activities after school
- parents teach their kids to be polite

TYPE OF LANGUAGE TO USE FOR YOUR ARGUMENT

- formal
- polite
- confident
- persuasive

Writing An Argument — 1

Use your best ideas from over the page to fill in the writing frame below.

What points will you make in your argument?

1. ....

2. ....

3. ....

What facts will you use to **back up** your argument?

1. ....
....

2. ....
....

3. ....
....

How will you **end** your argument? ....
....

*Rules for writing awesome **arguments** are on the flap at the back.*
Read the rules — then use your plan to write a mind-blowing argument.
Get ☐ rules right in your argument for a free pass to Writing Wonderland.

© CGP 2003

Section 1 — Writing An Argument

Writing An Argument — 2

Argument writing is always the same. Work out what the other person thinks and then argue like mad against them.

A letter from a parent to your school newsletter says:

"Children should be given more homework. They won't learn anything otherwise. They should have two hours every evening. This would also stop them from running around outside and causing a nuisance." (Mrs Smith)

Write a reply to the school newsletter arguing against these views.

You should consider:

- What points Mrs Smith makes which you disagree with
- What points you will make to argue against Mrs Smith
- Facts or examples you can include to support your argument

Put your own ideas for your argument in the boxes below.

WHAT MRS SMITH SAYS THAT YOU DON'T LIKE

kids should do more homework

kids shouldn't have free time to run around outside

REASONS KIDS SHOULDN'T HAVE MORE HOMEWORK

need time to have fun and make friends

playing outside is healthy

more homework would stop extra-curricular activities

GOOD THINGS KIDS DO INSTEAD OF HOMEWORK

swimming, football, reading, time with family, time with friends

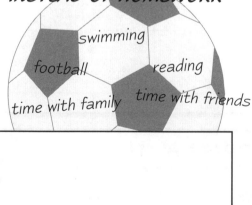

TYPE OF LANGUAGE YOU SHOULD USE

formal, indignant, confident, polite

Section 1 — Writing An Argument

Writing An Argument — 2

Now you can use your favourite ideas to fill in the writing frame below.

Write down **three points** Mrs Smith makes which **you disagree with**.

1. ....

2. ....

3. ....

Write down **three points** you can make to argue against Mrs Smith.

1. ....

2. ....

3. ....

Write down a **fact or example** to **back up** each of **your points** in the middle box.

1. ....

2. ....

3. ....

*Rules for writing awesome **arguments** are on the flap at the back.
Read the rules — then use your plan to write a mind-blowing argument.
Get ☐ rules right in your argument for a free pass to Writing Wonderland.*

Section 1 — Writing An Argument

Writing An Argument — 3

Here it is — the last time this book will give you an official excuse to argue...

An article in a local magazine says:

"Zoos are really cruel — the enclosures are always really cramped and always have bars. Breeding programs for rare animals are just an excuse to keep animals locked up. Plus, no one enjoys looking at animals — it's really boring."

Write a reply to the magazine arguing in support of zoos.

You should decide:
- What points in the article you disagree with
- What points you can make in support of zoos
- What examples and facts you can use to back up your argument

Put extra ideas in the boxes below — remember to be <u>formal</u> and <u>polite</u>.

WHAT THE ARTICLE SAYS THAT YOU DON'T AGREE WITH
- breeding programs aren't useful
- enclosures are always cramped

REASONS YOU LIKE GOING TO THE ZOO
- good day out
- see interesting animals close-up
- learn about different animals

EXAMPLES OF GOOD ANIMAL ENCLOSURES YOU'VE SEEN
- enclosure that look like real habitat
- climbing frames and trees for the monkeys
- lemurs and birds wander around freely
- big enclosures

REASONS BREEDING PROGRAMS ARE GOOD
- some species might die out
- breeding programs mean more endangered animals are born
- protected place for the endangered animals

Section 1 — Writing An Argument

Writing An Argument — 3

Now fill in the splendiferous writing frame below, using ideas from over the page.

Write down the **three main points** in the article that you disagree with.

1. ....
2. ....
3. ....

Write down **three points** you can make to argue against the points in the article.

1. ....
2. ....
3. ....

Write down a **fact or example** to **back up** each of **your points** in the middle box.

1. ....
2. ....
3. ....

Rules for writing awesome **arguments** are on the flap at the back.
Read the rules — then use your plan to write a mind-blowing argument.
Get ☐ rules right in your argument for a free pass to Writing Wonderland.

Section 1 — Writing An Argument

Section 2 — Recounting Events

Recounting Events — 1

Where? Who? When? How? Phew! What a lot of things to remember...

You have witnessed a handbag snatch on your local high street and the police are interviewing witnesses to gather evidence.

Recount the events to the police, making sure you include as many important facts as you can to help them catch the thief.

You will need to include:

- Where and when the snatch took place
- What the thief looked like
- What happened next

Write down all your own ideas for the account here.
Remember to include as many details as possible.

THINGS TO DESCRIBE ABOUT THE THIEF

age   clothes   height
build   hair colour

POSSIBLE LOCATIONS

outside a supermarket
leaving a restaurant

THINGS YOU MIGHT HAVE DONE

rushed over to help the victim   chased the thief but lost him   nothing

Recounting Events — 1

Here's the writing grid — choose your favourite ideas from the opposite page to fill it in.

Where and **when** did the snatch take place? ....

....

What did the thief **look like**?

What did you see **happen**?

What did you **do**?

*Rules for writing admirable **accounts** are on the flap at the back.
Read the rules — then use your plan to write an account that doesn't miss a trick.
Get ☐ rules right in your account for a free pass to Writing Wonderland.*

Section 2 — Recounting Events

Recounting Events — 2

Have a good gossip — tell your friend all the juicy details.

Something happened to you on your way home from school last night.

Recount the event to your best friend.

You will need to decide:
- Where and when the event took place
- Who else was there
- What happened

Write down extra ideas in the boxes below.

POSSIBLE EVENTS
- you witnessed a crime
- you bumped into an old friend
- you saw a deer

OTHER PEOPLE
- an old friend
- your mum
- a paramedic

DETAILS TO INCLUDE
- things you said
- what you saw
- what a person looked like

WHAT HAPPENED AT THE END
- you ended up with a broken toe
- you got the address of your old friend and promised to write to them

Section 2 — Recounting Events

Recounting Events — 2

Plan your account here. Include as many details as you can.

When and where did the event take place?

What happened?

Who else was with you? ....

....

What did you **do**?

*Rules for writing admirable **accounts** are on the flap at the back.
Read the rules — then use your plan to write an account that doesn't miss a trick.
Get ☐ rules right in your account for a free pass to Writing Wonderland.*

Recounting Events — 3

Recounting — it's all in the detail.

You have witnessed a fight in the playground at school. Your teacher wants to find out exactly what happened.

Recount to your teacher the events of the fight.

You will need to include:

- Who was involved
- What you saw
- What you heard
- What you did

Scribble down all your ideas. Give as much information as you can.

WHO WAS FIGHTING

- two of your friends
- people you don't know from the year below you

WHAT THEY WERE FIGHTING ABOUT

- one had been bullying the other's best friend
- one had been calling the other names

THINGS YOU MIGHT HAVE DONE

- stepped in to break it up
- got a member of staff
- joined in for fun

Section 2 — Recounting Events

Recounting Events — 3

Use your favourite ideas from the opposite page to fill in the writing grid below.

Who was involved in the fight?

What did you **see** and **hear** happen?

What did you **do**?

Rules for writing admirable **accounts** are on the flap at the back.
Read the rules — then use your plan to write an account that doesn't miss a trick.
Get ☐ rules right in your account for a free pass to Writing Wonderland.

Section 2 — Recounting Events

Section 3 — Articles

Articles — 1

If you want to be a journalist, pay attention. If you want to pass your SAT, pay attention. Every single blimmin' one of you, pay attention.

Your school has just started a weekly newsletter and they need students to write articles for it.

Write an article for the school newsletter — it could be a sports article or an article about an event that has happened in school.

You will need to think about:
- What event the article is about
- What facts to write about
- What quotes to include

Remember you have to be unbiased and describe things fairly. Save your opinion for the conclusion.

POSSIBLE EVENTS

netball final
headteacher's leaving assembly
teachers v. kids football match
the school's Christmas show

THINGS THAT HAPPENED DURING THE EVENT

who scored goals
who won the match
who gave speeches
who performed well

PEOPLE TO QUOTE

a teacher says...
a pupil says...
the headteacher says...
a parent says...

GOOD WORDS TO DESCRIBE THE EVENT

sad
entertaining
funny
energetic
exciting
ridiculous

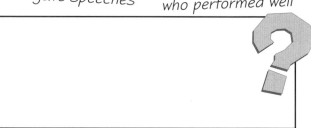

Articles — 1

Now fill in this writing plan, using your best ideas from the last page.

What event are you writing about? ....

....

What facts will you write about?	**What quotes** will you include?

How will you **end** your article? ....

....

Rules for writing arresting **articles** are on the flap at the back.
Read the rules — then use your plan to write an article that's feisty but fair.
Get ☐ rules right in your account for a free pass to Writing Wonderland.

Articles — 2

Now you're nearly Superman — when he's not flying, he writes articles just like you.

A local newspaper has invited pupils from your school to write an article about a school trip.

Write an article for the local newspaper describing a school trip.

You should include:
- Where the trip was to
- What you did when you were there
- Different opinions about the place you went to

Just because you need to be fair and unbiased doesn't mean you have to be boring. Include lots of weird words and fancy phrases to keep your reader awake.

PLACES FOR THE SCHOOL TRIP

wildlife park, theatre, museum, festival

WORDS TO DESCRIBE THE TRIP

informative, fascinating, entertaining, educational, unusual

WHAT YOU DID DURING THE TRIP

watched a play, did a quiz, saw musical and dance performances

PEOPLE YOU COULD QUOTE ABOUT THE TRIP

museum/park guide, teacher, other pupils, other visitors

Articles — 2

Bet even Superman had to mess about with writing frames...

Where was the school trip to? ....
....

What did you do during the trip?

What **opinions and quotes** about the trip will you include in your article?

What is your **conclusion** about the trip? ....
....
....

> Rules for writing arresting **articles** are on the flap at the back.
> Read the rules — then use your plan to write an article that's feisty but fair.
> Get ☐ rules right in your account for a free pass to Writing Wonderland.

Articles — 3

Keep at it. Practice, as some nincompoop once said, makes perfect.

There is a competition in a local newspaper to write an article about a local event.

Write an article about a local event for the competition.

You will need to decide on:
- What event you are going to write about
- What happened during the event
- Different opinions and quotes about the event

Remember try and make your article interesting, unbiased and informative.

LOCAL EVENTS
- regatta
- fairground
- big football match
- switching on Christmas lights

THINGS THAT HAPPENED AT THE EVENT
- mayor opened it
- local star won lots of races
- big crowd turned up
- different rides

WORDS TO DESCRIBE THE EVENT
- exciting
- dazzling
- friendly
- entertaining

WHO YOU COULD QUOTE ABOUT THE EVENT
- parents
- speakers at the event
- friends

Articles — 3

Now you've had a think, try filling in this writing frame for your article.

What local event are you going to write about? ....

....

What happened during the event?

What quotes will you include?

What is your **conclusion** about the event? ....

....

....

*Rules for writing arresting **articles** are on the flap at the back.
Read the rules — then use your plan to write an article that's feisty but fair.
Get ☐ rules right in your account for a free pass to Writing Wonderland.*

Section 4 — Biographies

Biographies — 1

People are pretty darned interesting don't you think? Yup, time to write about them then...

> **Write a biography about the achievements of someone (person or animal) close to you.**
>
> You will need to decide:
> - Who you are writing about
> - What they have achieved
> - How to make it interesting to read
> - How to finish the biography

Scribble down your ideas here.
Remember, you need to write about someone's entire life, not just a small part of it.

WHO YOU COULD WRITE ABOUT

your grandma   your pet

your dad   your best friend

SORTS OF THINGS THEY MIGHT HAVE ACHIEVED

helped people as part of their job   done work for charity

lived to be 100   played a musical instrument

HOW TO END THE BIOGRAPHY

how you remember them best

their favourite saying

looking towards the future

Biographies — 1

Plan your biography here, and make it juicy.

Who is your biography about? ....

What are their **achievements**?

What subheadings will you use?

How will the biography **end**?

Rules for writing brilliant **biographies** are on the flap at the back.
Read the rules — then use your plan to write a rivetingly revealing biography.
Get ☐ rules right in your biography for a free pass to Writing Wonderland.

Section 4 — Biographies

Biographies — 2

Now it's time to embarrass one of your closest friends... Ho ho ho...

Write a biography about one of your friends from school.

You will need to include:
- Who you are writing about
- Where and when they were born
- What interesting things they have done
- How to finish the biography

Try and make it interesting to someone who doesn't know the person.

POSSIBLE BIG EVENTS TO MENTION

moving house

getting a new baby brother

SORTS OF THINGS THEY MIGHT HAVE DONE

played the lead in a play

played an instrument

been to France

HOW TO END THE BIOGRAPHY

how they feel about moving up to secondary school

any plans for the future

Section 4 — Biographies

Biographies — 2

Use this writing frame to help you plan your little embarrassing piece.

Who are you writing about? ....

Where and **when** were they **born**? ....

....

What interesting things have they done?

What subheadings will you use?

How will the biography **end**?

*Rules for writing brilliant **biographies** are on the flap at the back. Read the rules — then use your plan to write a rivetingly revealing biography. Get ☐ rules right in your biography for a free pass to Writing Wonderland.*

Section 4 — Biographies

Section 5 — Newsletters

Newsletters — 1

And the breaking news is... it's time you had a go at writing a newsletter.

St Barnabus Primary School is holding a talent competition.

The Headteacher wants to invite as many parents and members of the community as possible to raise funds for the school.

He has asked the children to promote the competition using a newsletter.

Imagine you are a Year 6 pupil at the school.
Your task is to write a newsletter promoting the talent contest.

Write your ideas for the newsletter in the boxes.
Don't be shy — make them as crazy as you like.

GUEST STARS

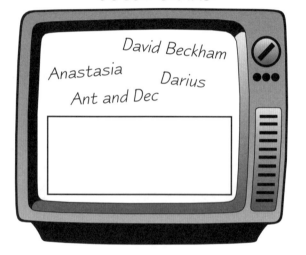

David Beckham
Anastasia
Darius
Ant and Dec

EXTRA EVENTS

worst adult singer
guess the weight of the headteacher
welly throwing

PERSUASIVE AND POWERFUL WORDS AND PHRASES

outstanding talent
not to be missed
awesome
valuable prizes
world famous celebrity

PRIZES TO BE WON

season ticket to Old Trafford
one year free cinema pass
visit to set of next Harry Potter film

Newsletters — 1

Here's the writing frame — use your favourite ideas from the opposite page.

When is it happening? ....

Where is it happening? ....

Who is invited? ....

....

What will happen at the event?	**Why** should parents come?

*Rules for writing noteworthy **newsletters** are on the flap at the back.*
Read the rules — then use your plan to write a newsletter that draws the reader in.
Get ☐ rules right in your biography for a free pass to Writing Wonderland.

Section 5 — Newsletters

Newsletters — 2

Can I persuade you to write another newsletter?

Imagine that you are a member of a club at your school. To attract new members, the club has decided to advertise using a newsletter.

**Write a newsletter to promote your club
and to encourage new members.**

You will need to include:
- The name of the club and a brief description of what it does
- Reasons why people should join
- Any upcoming events

*Write all your ideas down here.
Think about how you will make your club sound fun.*

POSSIBLE CLUBS
- drama
- school radio
- Harry Potter fanclub

REASONS FOR JOINING
- weekly meetings of the club
- can take part in all club activities
- free badge

POSSIBLE EVENTS
- play
- disco
- visit from J. K. Rowling

Section 5 — Newsletters

Newsletters — 2

Use this writing frame to help you plan your newsletter.

What is the **name** of your club? ....

....

What does your club **do**?

Why should people join your club?

What events does the club have planned?

Rules for writing noteworthy **newsletters** are on the flap at the back.
Read the rules — then use your plan to write a newsletter that draws the reader in.
Get ☐ rules right in your biography for a free pass to Writing Wonderland.

Section 5 — Newsletters

Newsletters — 3

Get your persuading hat on... you've got another newsletter to write.

Your school is organising a sponsored 12-hour dance-athon for charity.

Write a newsletter to encourage people to take part in the event.

You should include:

- When and where it will take place
- Which charity the proceeds will be going to
- Why people should take part
- How to sponsor someone

Write down your ideas in these boxes.

POSSIBLE CHARITIES

NSPCC

The International Red Cross

REASONS TO TAKE PART

it is for a very good cause

it will be fun

WHAT PEOPLE CAN DO

take part in the dancing

sponsor someone else to dance

PERSUASIVE AND POWERFUL PHRASES

every penny raised could make a difference

charity event of the year

Section 5 — Newsletters

Newsletters — 3

Plan your newsletter here. Use the ideas you like best from over the page.

Which charity will the proceeds go to? ....

When and **where** will the dance-athon take place?

Why should people take part?

How can people sponsor someone taking part?

*Rules for writing noteworthy **newsletters** are on the flap at the back.
Read the rules — then use your plan to write a newsletter that draws the reader in.
Get ☐ rules right in your biography for a free pass to Writing Wonderland.*

Section 6 — Instructions

Instructions — 1

Try writing some instructions — make them clear, so even the most dopey person gets them.

> Imagine that a friend is coming to your house for tea and basketball practice. He or she hasn't lived in the area long and needs to know how to get to your house.
>
> **Write out some instructions that your friend can understand.**
>
> You will need to decide:
> - Where your friend is coming from
> - How many steps to break up the instructions into
> - What language to use to make the instructions clear

Write down your ideas for your instructions in the boxes below.

THINGS ON THE ROUTE

field of cows, blue house, laundrette, corner shop

WHEN TO WRITE A NEW INSTRUCTION

every time they have to turn, when the road name changes, every 200 metres or so

DIRECTING WORDS

Turn right...
Continue straight ahead
Look out for...
Watch out for the...

Section 6 — Instructions

Instructions — 1

Use your best ideas from the opposite page to fill in the writing frame.

How should your friend get to your house?

How many steps will the instructions break up into?

How will you **separate** each step of the instructions?

What kind of **language** will you use? ....

....

*Rules for writing ingenious **instructions** are on the flap at the back.
Read the rules — then use your plan to write instructions that even I would follow.
Get ☐ rules right in your biography for a free pass to Writing Wonderland.*

Section 6 — Instructions

Instructions — 2

Instructions are great — they make people do as you say, which is always a good thing.

Imagine that your friend is looking after your hamster whilst you are on holiday.

**Write some instructions for your friend that tell him
how to care for your hamster for one week.**

You will need to decide:

- How often the hamster needs feeding, handling and cleaning out
- What it eats and drinks
- How to break up the instructions into different steps

Put your ideas in the boxes below — think about how you're going to break up the instructions.

POSSIBLE NAMES FOR YOUR HAMSTER

Flump, Wilfred, Ruby-Rose

THINGS THE HAMSTER NEEDS

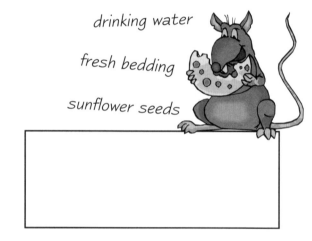

drinking water, fresh bedding, sunflower seeds

WAYS TO HANDLE THE HAMSTER

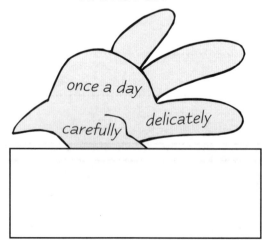

once a day, carefully, delicately

WAYS TO BREAK UP THE INSTRUCTIONS

new instruction for each new day

...for each different task (e.g. feeding, cleaning...)

Section 6 — Instructions

Instructions — 2

Here's the writing frame — plan your instructions in it using your ideas from the boxes.

What does your friend need to do about...

...feeding?

...cleaning out?

...handling?

What does your hamster need to **eat** and **drink?**

How will you **break up** the instructions into different **steps?** ....

....

....

*Rules for writing ingenious **instructions** are on the flap at the back.*
Read the rules — then use your plan to write instructions that even I could follow.
Get ☐ rules right in your biography for a free pass to Writing Wonderland.

Section 6 — Instructions

Instructions — 3

One last set of instructions to write — don't blame me, I'm just following instructions.

You have an alien staying at your house — it doesn't know anything about humans.

Write some instructions for the alien, telling it how to make a cup of tea. You will have to explain every tiny detail.

You will need to think about:

- What steps are involved in making a cup of tea
- How to explain every tiny detail (e.g. what a teabag looks like etc)
- How to break up the instructions into different steps

Put your ideas into the boxes — remember that this alien doesn't know <u>anything</u> about making tea, so make your instructions really detailed.

POSSIBLE STEPS

pouring water into a mug

putting the kettle on

THINGS THAT NEED DESCRIBING

sugar
teabag
kettle

PHRASES TO USE

move the spoon in circles round the mug

carefully pour...

Section 6 — Instructions

Instructions — 3

Fill in the writing frame with your best ideas — remember to have detailed steps.

What steps are involved in making tea?

What things needed for making tea do you need to **describe**? ....

....

....

How will you describe them?

How will you **break up** the instructions into different **steps**? ....

....

....

....

Rules for writing ingenious **instructions** are on the flap at the back.
Read the rules — then use your plan to write instructions that even I could follow.
Get ☐ rules right in your instructions for a free pass to Writing Wonderland.

Section 7 — Descriptions

Descriptions — 1

For this one you've got to describe your teacher — don't be mean.

Your parents want to meet your teacher at the school sports day but they're not sure what he or she looks like.

Write a description of your teacher, so your parents can easily recognise him or her. Include appearance and personality in your description.

You will need to think about:
- What your teacher looks like
- What kind of personality your teacher has
- How to help your parents imagine exactly what your teacher looks like.

Good descriptions pick out things that are unusual and interesting. Try and think of a few really attention-grabbing points to put in your description.

WHAT YOUR TEACHER LOOKS LIKE

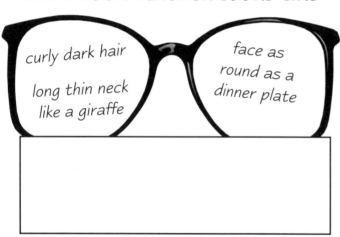

- curly dark hair
- long thin neck like a giraffe
- face as round as a dinner plate

WHAT YOUR TEACHER WEARS

- tweed suit
- diving suit
- purple velvet tracksuit

WHAT YOUR TEACHER'S PERSONALITY IS LIKE

- stern and serious
- grumpy on Mondays, nice the rest of the time
- likes scary stuff like hang gliding and bungee jumping

WHAT HABITS YOUR TEACHER HAS

- drums fingers on desk
- stands up very straight
- waves arms around a lot
- tells really bad jokes

Descriptions — 1

Use the grid to firm up your ideas. Decide exactly which points you're going to include in your description.

Who are you writing about? ....

What does he or she **look** like?

What is his or her **personality** like?

Rules for writing delicious **descriptions** are on the flap at the back.
Read the rules — then use your plan to write a description that paints a picture.
Get ☐ rules right in your description for a free pass to Writing Wonderland.

© CGP 2003

Section 7 — Descriptions

Descriptions — 2

They could get you to describe just about anything in the SAT. Even a supermarket.

Your Chinese penfriend has sent you a description of the city where she lives.

Write a description of places you know well, in the city, town or village where you live, for your penfriend.

You will need to think about:

- Which places to describe
- What they look like
- What you do there
- How to make your description clear and interesting for somebody who has never been to the place you are describing

If you don't know what to write about, try and imagine you were visiting the place where you live for the first time and what you would notice.

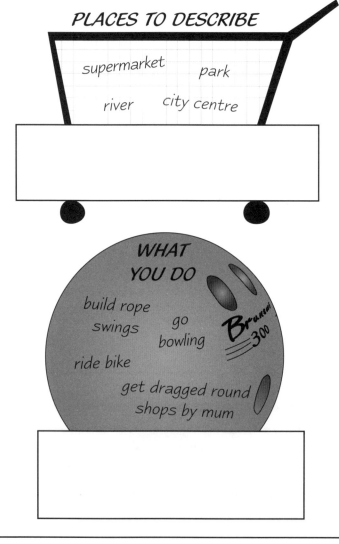

PLACES TO DESCRIBE

supermarket   park
river   city centre

WHAT YOU DO

build rope swings   go bowling
ride bike
get dragged round shops by mum

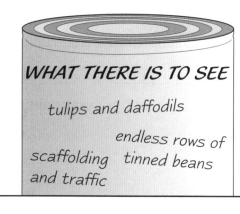

WHAT THERE IS TO SEE

tulips and daffodils
endless rows of
scaffolding   tinned beans
and traffic

THINGS YOU MIGHT NEED TO EXPLAIN TO YOUR PENFRIEND

what kind of   cars drive on
clothes people wear   the left
what people eat

Section 7 — Descriptions

Descriptions — 2

Take all your best ideas from the opposite page and fit them into this writing frame so you'll know exactly what to say in your description.

What is the **name** of the city, town or village you are writing about?

....

Which three places are you going to describe, and what are you going to say about them?

1.

2.

3.

What language will you use to make your description clear and interesting?

---

*Rules for writing delicious **descriptions** are on the flap at the back.*
Read the rules — then use your plan to write a description that paints a picture.
Get ☐ rules right in your description for a free pass to Writing Wonderland.

Section 8 — Explanations

Explanations — 1

Time to explain the mysteries of the universe... or at least the mysteries of the water cycle.

Year 4 are learning about the water cycle but have lost the class science book that explains how it works.

Write an explanation of the water cycle for Year 4 and explain any technical words that they may not know.

You will need to decide:

- What the main facts you need to include are
- What technical words to include
- How to lay out your explanation

Don't despair — you don't have to write a Nobel-prize-winning piece. Stick to simple facts that Year 4s would find easy to understand. Get the facts straight here.

WHAT THE MAIN STEPS OF THE WATER CYCLE ARE

1. water in rivers, lakes, sea
2. Sun makes water evaporate

TRICKY WORDS THAT YEAR 4 MIGHT NOT KNOW

evaporate   cycle

MAIN SECTIONS OF YOUR EXPLANATION

glossary
introduction
fish tank

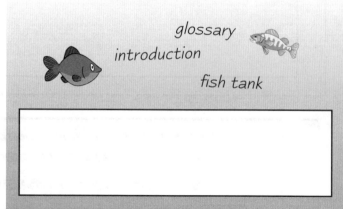

Explanations — 1

This is a tricky topic, so make sure you get your ideas really well organised before you start writing.

What facts will you include?

What technical words will you use?

What will your **subheadings** be?

....

....

....

*Rules for writing enviable **explanations** are on the flap at the back.
Read the rules — then use your plan to write an exam-tastic explanation.
Get ▢ rules right in your explanation for a free pass to Writing Wonderland.*

Section 8 — Explanations

Explanations — 2

Give your explaining muscles a good workout with this question.

Many games have complicated rules. When somebody is learning to play a new game for the first time they need to have the rules explained to them.

Imagine you are describing how to play a game you know well to somebody who has never played it before. Write the explanation.

You will need to decide:

- What the rules are
- What order to explain them in
- What technical words you will need to explain

Use the space below to work out what game to describe and what to say about it.

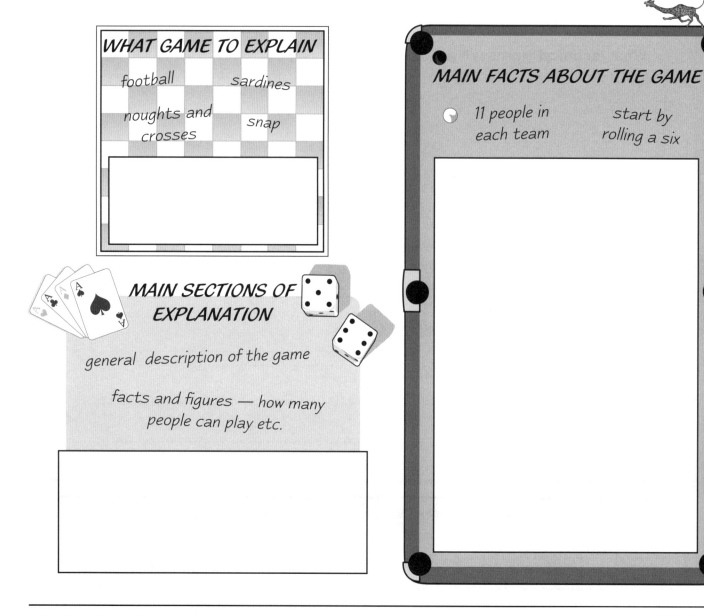

WHAT GAME TO EXPLAIN

football   sardines

noughts and crosses   snap

MAIN SECTIONS OF EXPLANATION

general description of the game

facts and figures — how many people can play etc.

MAIN FACTS ABOUT THE GAME

11 people in each team   start by rolling a six

Section 8 — Explanations

Explanations — 2

Now you've spent all this time thinking about playing games, you'd probably rather be playing them than writing about them. Well, tough. Plan your explanation here.

What game are you describing?

....

What rules will you cover in your explanation?

What technical words will you use?

What will your **subheadings** be?

....

....

....

*Rules for writing enviable **explanations** are on the flap at the back.
Read the rules — then use your plan to write an exam-tastic explanation.
Get ☐ rules right in your explanation for a free pass to Writing Wonderland.*

Section 8 — Explanations

Explanations — 3

You could get asked to explain something really simple. Like brushing your teeth.

If aliens from outer space came to Earth they would find normal things we do, like brushing our teeth, very strange.

Aliens have invaded your bathroom. They have never seen somebody brushing their teeth before and they want you to explain what you are doing and why. Write the explanation.

You will need to decide:
- What the main facts you need to include are
- What words to explain
- How to set out your explanation

Even though brushing your teeth is pretty simple you'll still need to give a really full explanation. Put lots of detail to make sure your explanation's good.

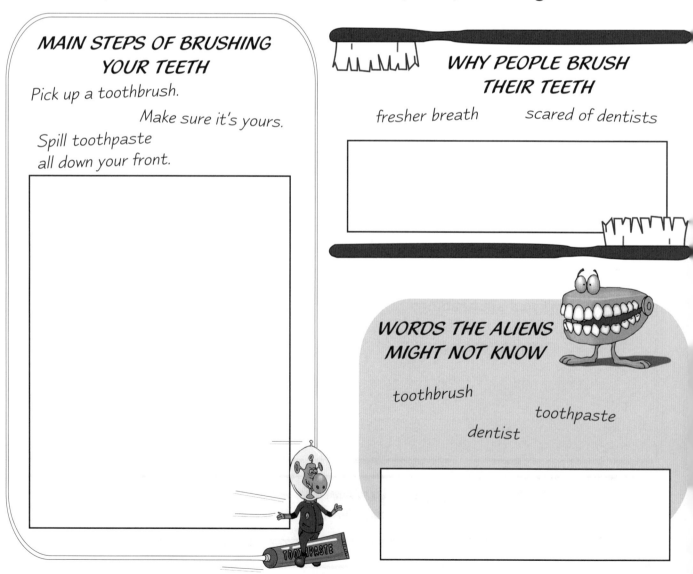

MAIN STEPS OF BRUSHING YOUR TEETH

Pick up a toothbrush.

Make sure it's yours.

Spill toothpaste all down your front.

WHY PEOPLE BRUSH THEIR TEETH

fresher breath   scared of dentists

WORDS THE ALIENS MIGHT NOT KNOW

toothbrush

toothpaste

dentist

Section 8 — Explanations

Explanations — 3

Hmmm... brushing your teeth. Don't you think it's fascinating that we brush our teeth every single day, but remembering exactly how we do it is really hard. Weird that...

What facts will you include about **how** to brush your teeth?

What facts will you include about **why** people brush their teeth?

What technical words will you explain?

What will your **subheadings** be?

....

....

*Rules for writing enviable **explanations** are on the flap at the back.*
Read the rules — then use your plan to write an exam-tastic explanation.
Get ☐ rules right in your explanation for a free pass to Writing Wonderland.